# First World War
## and Army of Occupation
# War Diary
## France, Belgium and Germany

1 INDIAN CAVALRY DIVISION
Divisional Troops
Rouse's Brigade Royal Horse Artillery
1 September 1914 - 26 November 1914

WO95/1170/2

The Naval & Military Press Ltd
www.nmarchive.com
**Published in association with The National Archives**

Published by

## The Naval & Military Press Ltd

Unit 10 Ridgewood Industrial Park,

Uckfield, East Sussex,

TN22 5QE England

Tel: +44 (0) 1825 749494

www.naval-military-press.com

www.nmarchive.com

*This diary has been reprinted in facsimile from the original. Any imperfections are inevitably reproduced and the quality may fall short of modern type and cartographic standards.*

© **Crown Copyright**
**Images reproduced by permission of The National Archives, London, England, 2015.**

# Contents

| Document type | Place/Title | Date From | Date To |
|---|---|---|---|
| Heading | WO95/1170/2 | | |
| Heading | BEF 1 Ind. Cav. Div. Troops Rouse's Bde RHA 1914 Sept To 1914 Nov | | |
| War Diary | Amballa | 01/09/1914 | 30/09/1914 |
| Heading | War Diary of Headquarters, Rouses Horse Artillery Brigade Indian Expeditionary Force 1st Oct To 31 October 1914 Volume II | | |
| War Diary | Amballa | 01/10/1914 | 08/10/1914 |
| War Diary | Bombay | 09/10/1914 | 31/10/1914 |
| Heading | War Diary of Headquarters Rouse's Horse Artillery Brigade 1st Indian Cavalry Division From 1st To 30th November 1914 | | |
| War Diary | | 01/11/1914 | 26/11/1914 |

WO 95/11707/2

# BEF

## 1 IND. CAV. DIV. TROOPS

### Rouse's Bde RHA

#### 1914 Sept to 1914 Nov

Army Form C. 2118.

# WAR DIARY
or
## INTELLIGENCE SUMMARY.

(Erase heading not required.)

Rouse Brigade R.H.A

| Hour, Date, Place. | Summary of Events and Information. | Remarks and references to Appendices. |
|---|---|---|
| AMBALA | | |
| 8pm 1st September 1914 | Received orders to mobilize the Headquarters of 1st Brigade R.H.A for active service | |
| 2nd September | Mobilization commenced in accordance with Mobilization Regs & Field Service Manual for R.H.A Brigade (India) 1914. Wanted to complete Establishment | |
| | Peace Establishment | |
| | 1 Colonel (Lt Colonel H. ROUSE D.S.O) | |
| | 1 Adjutant (Capt. A.E. ERSKINE) | |
| | 1 R.S.M | 7 gunners |
| | 1 Trumpeter | 7 horses with saddlery |
| | 1 Sergeant Cook (dismounted) | |
| | 1 Clerk (dismounted) | |
| 3rd Sept | Usual mobilization routine | |
| 4th Sept | do | |
| 5th Sept | Information received that Colonel H. Rouse will command the R.H.A Brigade, consisting of "A" & "Q" Batteries, "B" & "C" Ammunition Columns. | |

Army Form C. 2118.

Persian Horse Artillery
Brigade

# WAR DIARY
or
# INTELLIGENCE SUMMARY.

(Erase heading not required.)

| Hour, Date, Place. | Summary of Events and Information. | Remarks and references to Appendices. |
|---|---|---|
| AMBALLA | | |
| 6th September 1914 | Usual mobilization routine | |
| 7th September | 7 Horses (with saddlery) to complete establishment arrived from "I" Ammunition Column RHA Lahore | |
| 8th September | Received instructions that all Officers might take 3 chargers with them instead of two | |
| 9th September | 7 Gunners RHA to complete establishment, taken on strength of Headquarters | |
| 10th | Usual mobilization routine | |
| 11th do | do | |
| 12th do | do | |
| 13th do | Reported to Division that mobilization was complete | |
| 14th September to 30 September | awaiting orders to concentrate | |

C. R. Hopkins
Adjutant
Persian Horse Brigade RHA

a96

121/2168

<u>Confidential</u>

War Diary

of

Headquarters, 1st I. Cav. Div.

Rouse's Horse Artillery Brigade

Indian Expeditionary Force
1st Oct to 31 October
from ~~1st September to 30th September~~
— 1914 —

Volume ~~II~~ ?

Vol II  Poona Brigade  Page I
R.H.A.
Indian Cavalry Division

# WAR DIARY
## or
## INTELLIGENCE SUMMARY.

Army Form C. 2118.

(Erase heading not required.)

Instructions regarding War Diaries and Intelligence Summaries are contained in F. S. Regs., Part II, and the Staff Manual respectively. Title pages will be prepared in manuscript.

| Hour, Date, Place. | Summary of Events and Information. | Remarks and references to Appendices. |
|---|---|---|
| AMBALLA | | |
| 1st to 3rd October 1914 | Awaiting orders to concentrate. | |
| 4th October 1914 | Received instructions that "A" Battery & "C" Ammunition Column are to be prepared to entrain on Wednesday 7th October. Time to be notified later. Trucks for Headquarters R.H.A. to be attached to "C" Ammunition Column train. | |
| 5th October 1914. | Orders received for "C" Amm Column to entrain at 22.26 Wednesday 7th inst. | |
| 6th October 1914 | "A" Battery entrained in two trains for Bombay. Officer Commanding :- Major A.O.B. Simpson-Baikie Captain M.M. Haynes Lieut. D.M. Walker Lieut. the Hon'ble T.H. Freemes Lieut. G.C. Richardson to join in France. | |

Page 2    Vol II

Army Form C. 2118.

# WAR DIARY or INTELLIGENCE SUMMARY.

(Erase heading not required.)

Instructions regarding War Diaries and Intelligence Summaries are contained in F. S. Regs., Part II, and the Staff Manual respectively. Title pages will be prepared in manuscript.

| Hour, Date, Place. | Summary of Events and Information. | Remarks and references to Appendices. |
|---|---|---|
| AMBALLA | | |
| 7th October 1914 | — Nil — | |
| 8th October 1914 | Headquarters R.H.A. and 'C' Ammunition Column entrained for Bombay. Lieut. J. E. White in command of 'C' Ammn. Col. R.H.A. | |
| BOMBAY | | |
| 9th October 1914 | 'a' Battery detrained at Bombay docks & proceeded to Camp. | |
| 10th October 1914 | 'a' Battery embarked on S.S. ITRIA. (Troopship No. 90) | |
| 11th October 1914 | 'C' Ammunition Column detrained at Bombay docks. Part of Column embarked on S.S. CHILKA<br>"  "  "  "  S.S. ITRIA<br>Patton "  "  "  S.S. LAOMEDON<br>and Ammunition Wagons on S.S. FRANZ FERDINAND the remainder proceeded to Camp. | |
| 12th October 1914 | — Nil — | |
| 13th October 1914 | Remainder of 'C' Ammunition Column embarked on | |

Vol II
Page 3
Army Form O. 2118.

# WAR DIARY
or
# INTELLIGENCE SUMMARY.

(Erase heading not required.)

| Hour, Date, Place. | Summary of Events and Information. | Remarks and references to Appendices. |
|---|---|---|
| BOMBAY 13th October Contd. | S.S. ARRATOON APCAR. <br><br> REMARKS <br><br> The embarkation arrangements for "C" Ammn. Column showed a complete ignorance of its composition & total disregard for its efficiency on arrival at the port of disembarkation. <br><br> 2/ Appendix A (attached) is a copy of Embarkation orders, wherein it will be seen that instead of issuing separate embarkation orders to each Brigade Ammn Column, arrangements were only made for the Embarkation of a Divisional Ammn. Column, a unit which did not exist at the time. <br><br> 3/ The Divisional Ammn. Col was then divided up among Seven (7) different ships. All tactical personnel were put on one boat with ammunition wagons of "C" Ammn.Col. had eventually to be placed on board a ship where there was no Ammunition Column man with them. <br><br> It is inconceivable that an Indian Cavalry Regiment or Battery should have been treated in the same way. | Appendix (A) |

Vol II  Page 4

Army Form C. 2118.

# WAR DIARY
## or
## INTELLIGENCE SUMMARY.

*(Erase heading not required.)*

Instructions regarding War Diaries and Intelligence Summaries are contained in F. S. Regs., Part II, and the Staff Manual respectively. Title pages will be prepared in manuscript.

| Hour, Date, Place. | Summary of Events and Information. | Remarks and references to Appendices. |
|---|---|---|
| BOMBAY | By sending all the British ranks on one ship, it was impossible to have European supervision over the various detachments.  The inevitable consequence is that the horses will not receive the same attention as they would under their own officers and the efficiency of the Ammunition Column on landing will suffer enormously in consequence. Considerable difficulty was also caused in rearranging baggage and winter clothing, most of this had to be done after the ships were in harbour.  Finally, chaos confusion is bound to take place at the Port of disembarkation much valuable time will be spent in collecting the various detachments.  4. It is therefore urgently recommended that in the future, an ammunition Column whether Divisional or Brigade, should be embarked as a unit like any other fighting unit. | |

Page 5

Army Form O. 2118.

Vol II

# WAR DIARY
## or
## INTELLIGENCE SUMMARY.

*(Erase heading not required.)*

| Hour, Date, Place. | Summary of Events and Information. | Remarks and references to Appendices. |
|---|---|---|
| BOMBAY | | |
| 5.30 p.m. 16th October 1914 | Convoy weighed anchor. Major N.A.D. Simpson - Baikie 18th Bde Commanding troops aboard S.S. ITRIA. | — |
| 16th Oct to 31 Oct/14 | Report on + progress of stores on voyage etc. see WAR DIARY of A Battery R.H.A. | |

Alrkone
Capt
Comm Ridge RHA
31 Oct/14

Confidential

War Diary

of

Headquarters
ROUSE'S Horse Artillery Brigade

1st Indian Cavalry Division

from 1st to 30th November

1914      121/2743

(Volume III)

Page 1

Head Quarters — Rhovi's Horse Artillery Brigade. Vol III

Army Form C. 2118.

# WAR DIARY
or
## INTELLIGENCE SUMMARY.
(Erase heading not required.)

Instructions regarding War Diaries and Intelligence Summaries are contained in F. S. Regs., Part II, and the Staff Manual respectively. Title pages will be prepared in manuscript.

| Hour, Date, Place. | Summary of Events and Information. | Remarks and references to Appendices. |
|---|---|---|
| 1st November | Convoy arrived at Port Said in morning, & left again in the afternoon. | — |
| 10th November | Arrived at Marseilles. | — |
| 11th November | Disembarked. Went into billet in the Village of La Penne. | — |
| 12th November | Lieut E.H. Villiers attached as Interpreter. | — |
| 13th November | Entrained at Marseilles | |
| 14th " | — | |
| 15th November | Arrived Orleans, went into camp of LES GROVES. | — |
| 16th " " | in pouring rain. very cold & wet. "A" Battery arrived in same camp. "Q" Battery in camp 8 miles off at "LA SOURCE". | — |
| 17th " " | Headquarters moved into French Cavalry Barracks | |
| 28th " " | Received orders that "B" & "C" Ammunition Columns in Camp at LES GROVES, were to come under the Orders of OC Rohini Brigade &c | — |

Headquarters – ROUSE's Horse Artillery Brigade. Vol III (continued) Page 2

Army Form C. 2118.

# WAR DIARY
## or
## INTELLIGENCE SUMMARY.

(Erase heading not required.)

| Hour, Date, Place. | Summary of Events and Information. | Remarks and references to Appendices. |
|---|---|---|
| 24th November | Issued (from Transport) one G.S. Wagon and one heavy draught horse. | — |
| 25th November | G.S. Wagon and the pair of draught horses returned as horses shewed signs of "pink eye". | — |

J. Erskine
Major
Adjutant
Rouse's Horse Artillery Brigade

30th Nov/14

www.ingramcontent.com/pod-product-compliance
Lightning Source LLC
Chambersburg PA
CBHW081253170426
43191CB00037B/2143